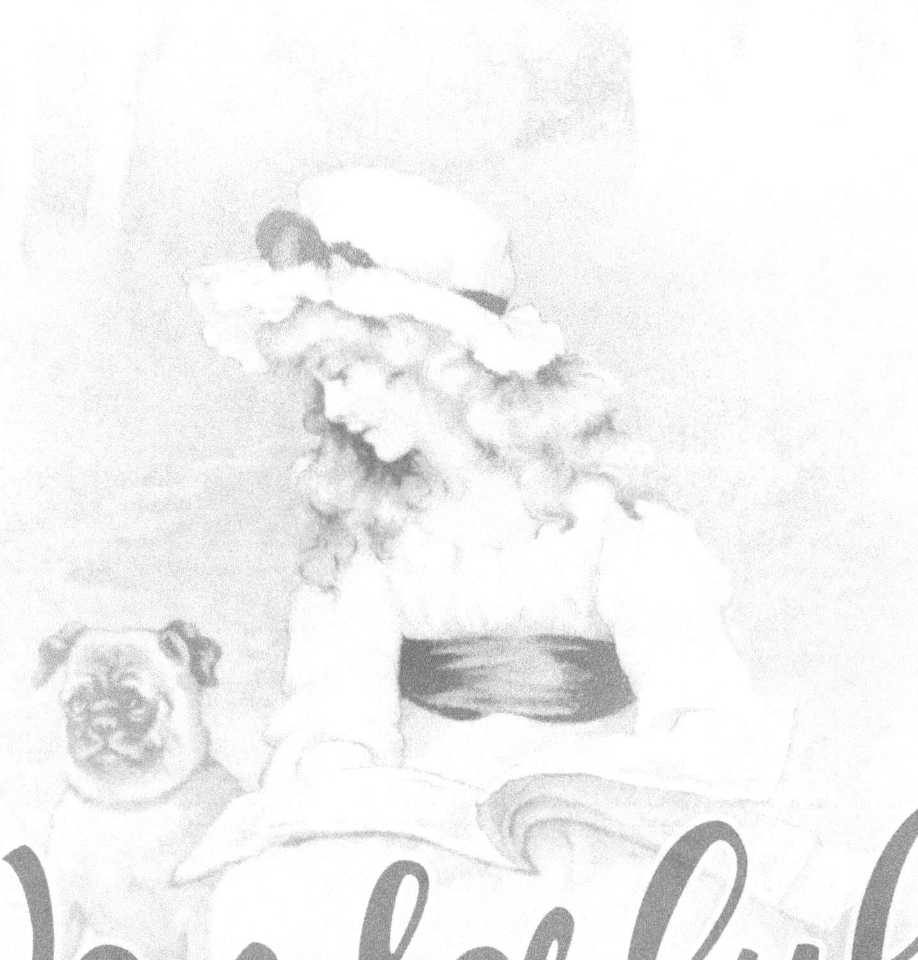

Wonderful childhood

Copyright 2020, All rights reserved

Wonderful Childhood

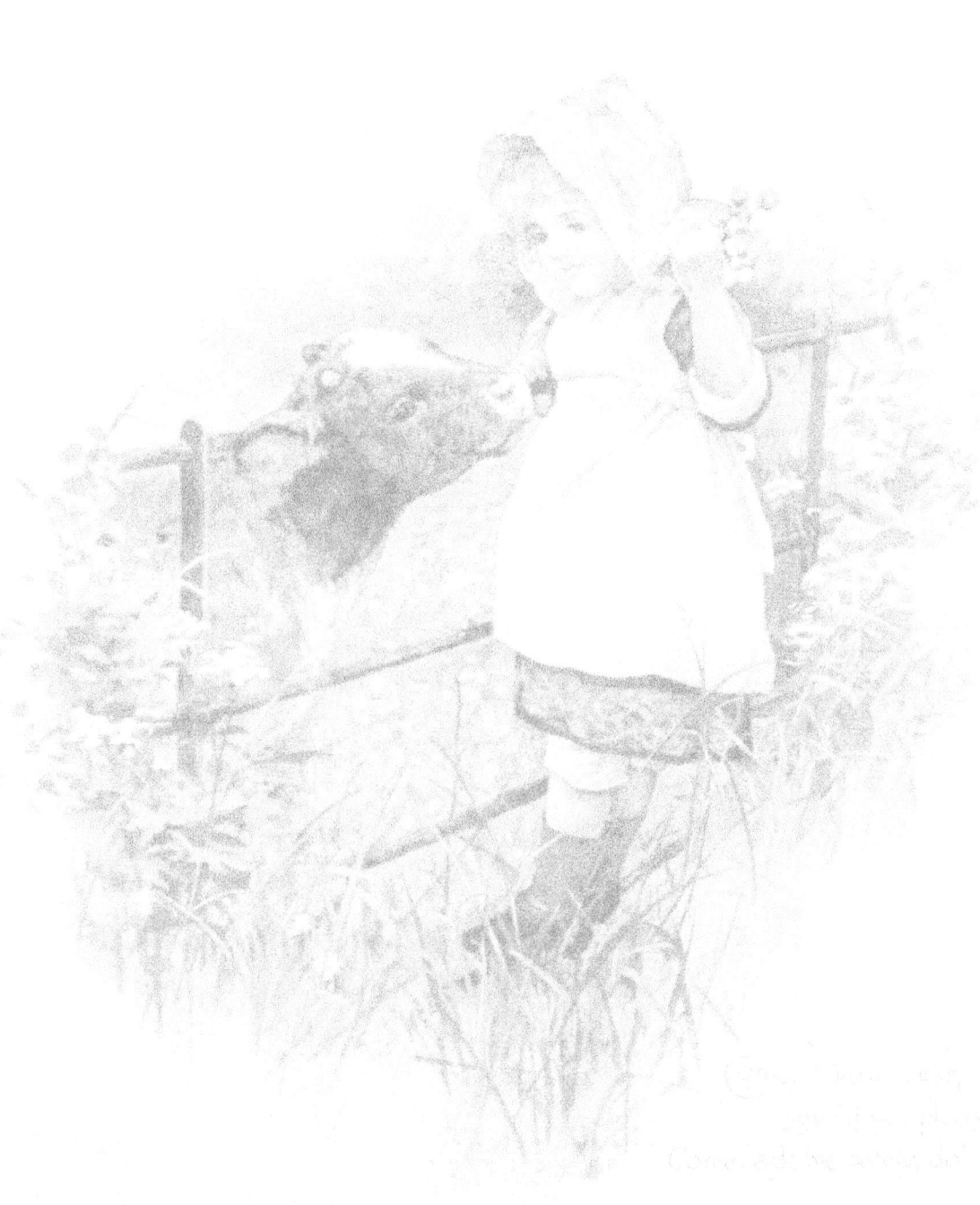

Wonderful Childhood

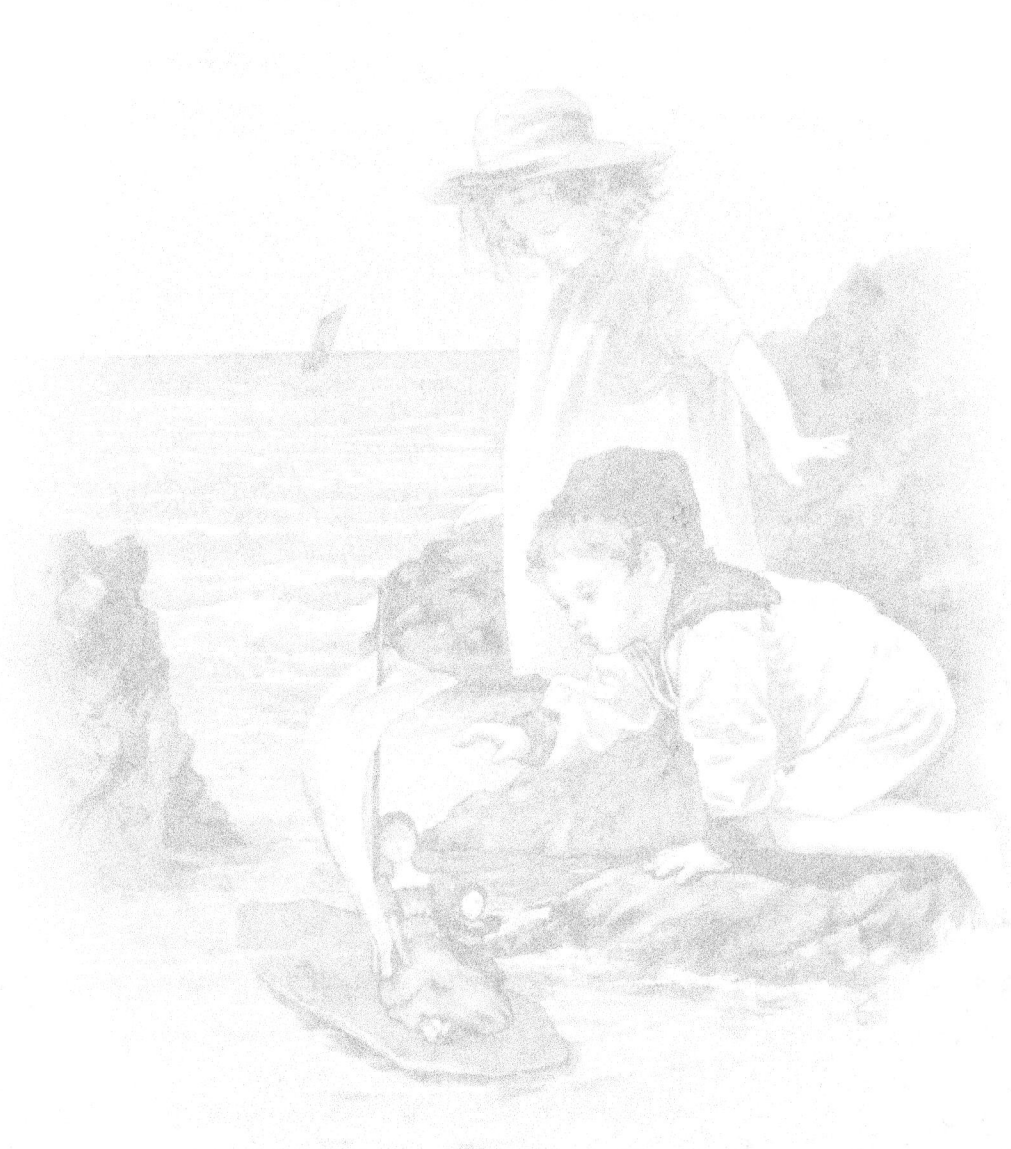

Wonderful Childhood

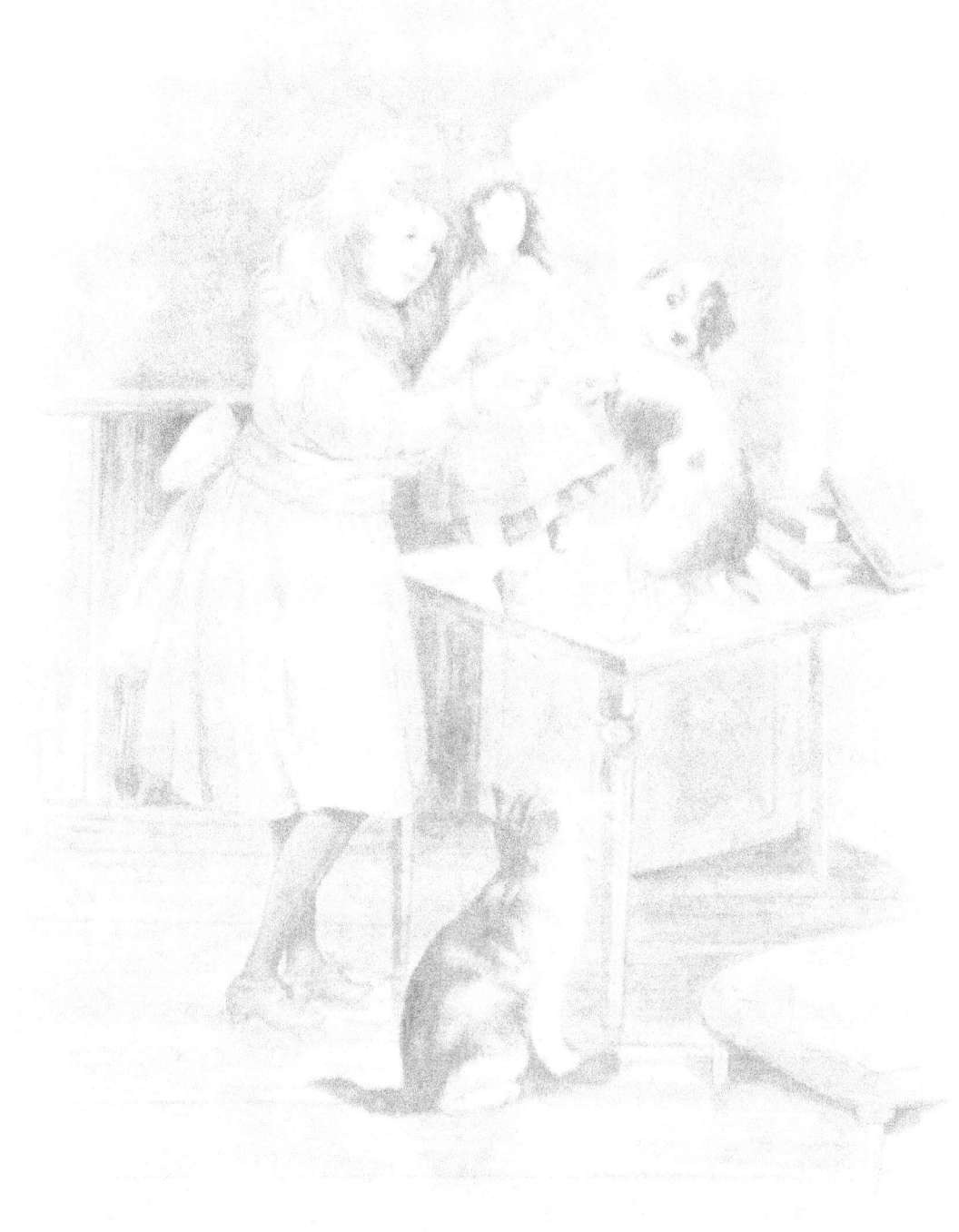

Wonderful Childhood

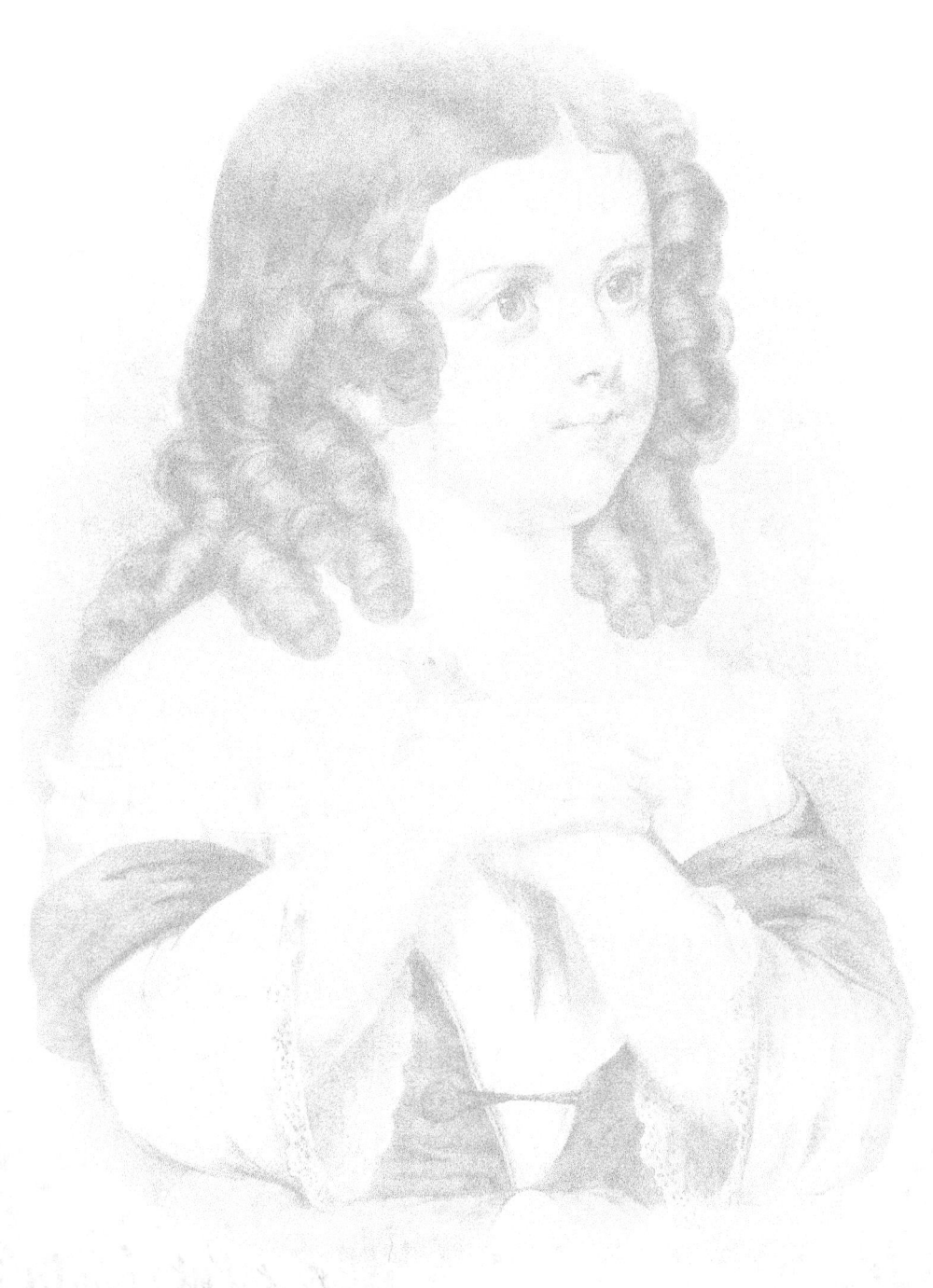

Wonderful Childhood

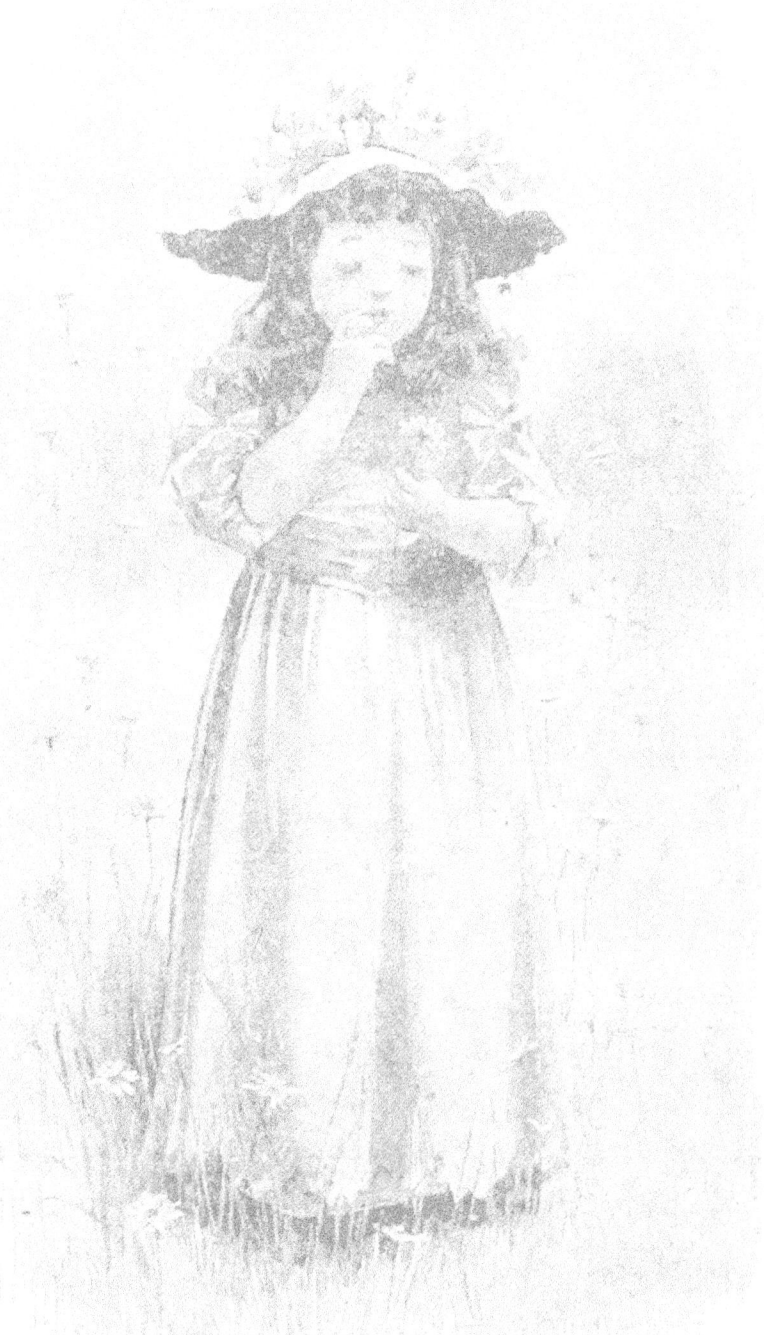

Wonderful Childhood

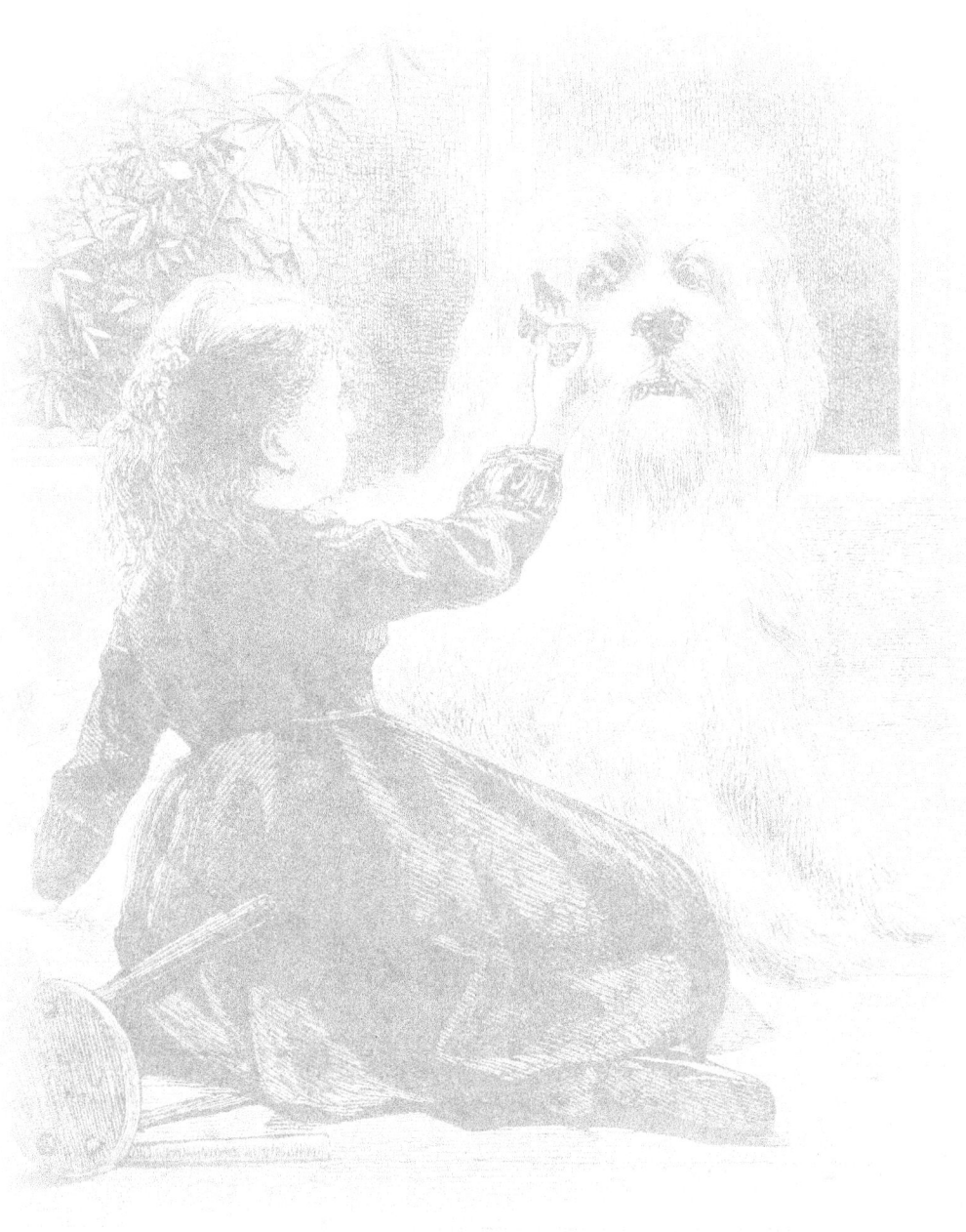

Wonderful Childhood

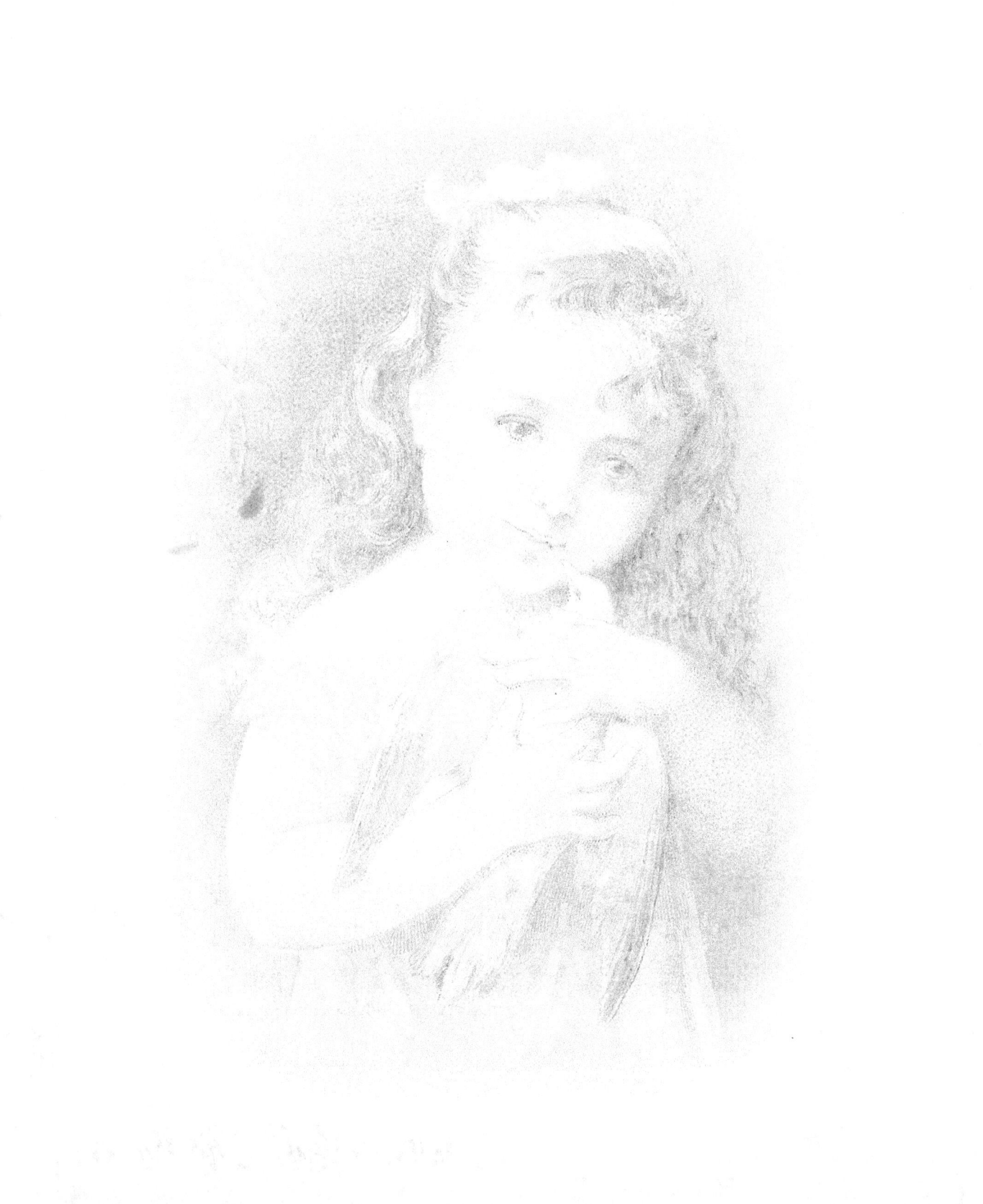

Wonderful Childhood

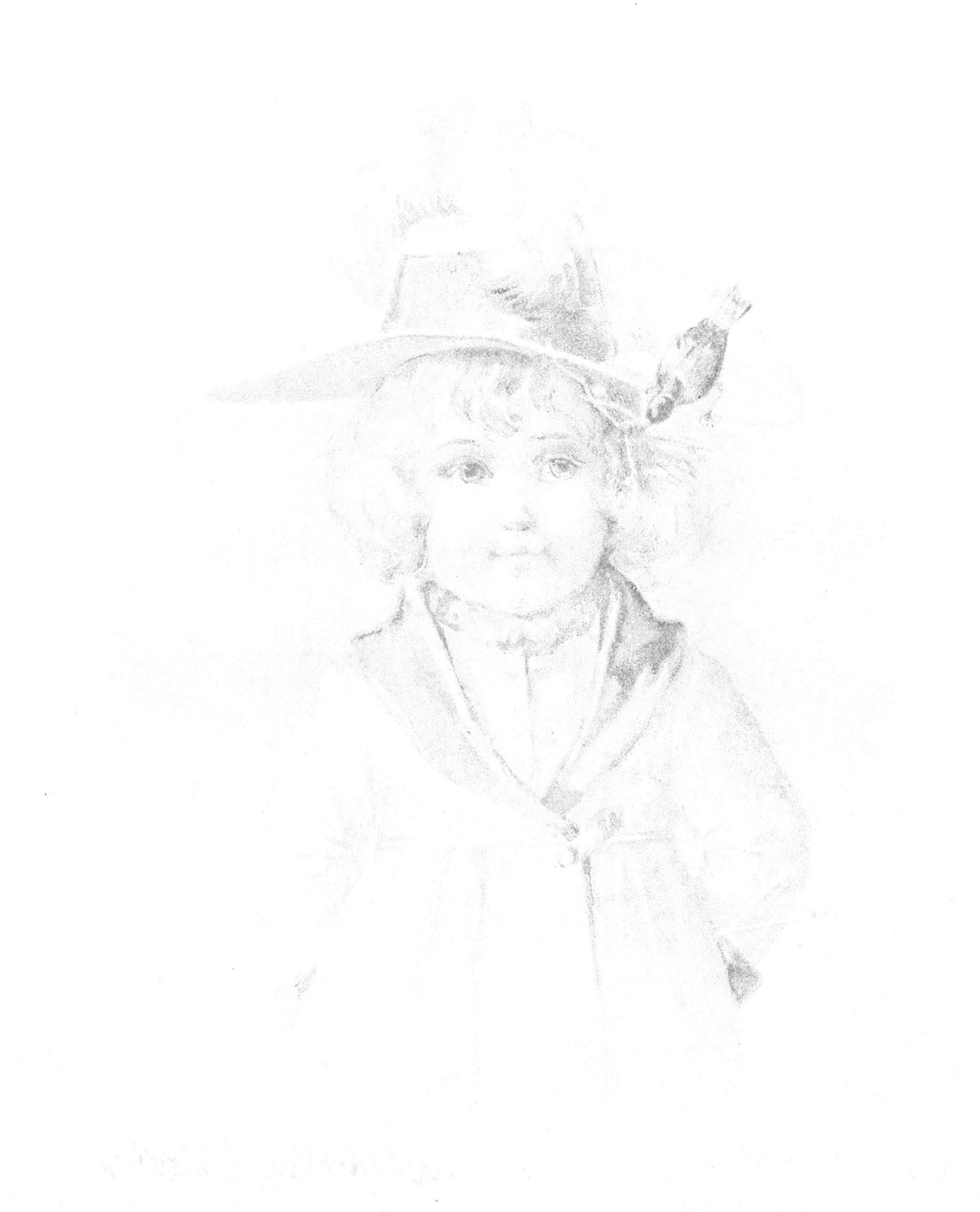

Wonderful Childhood

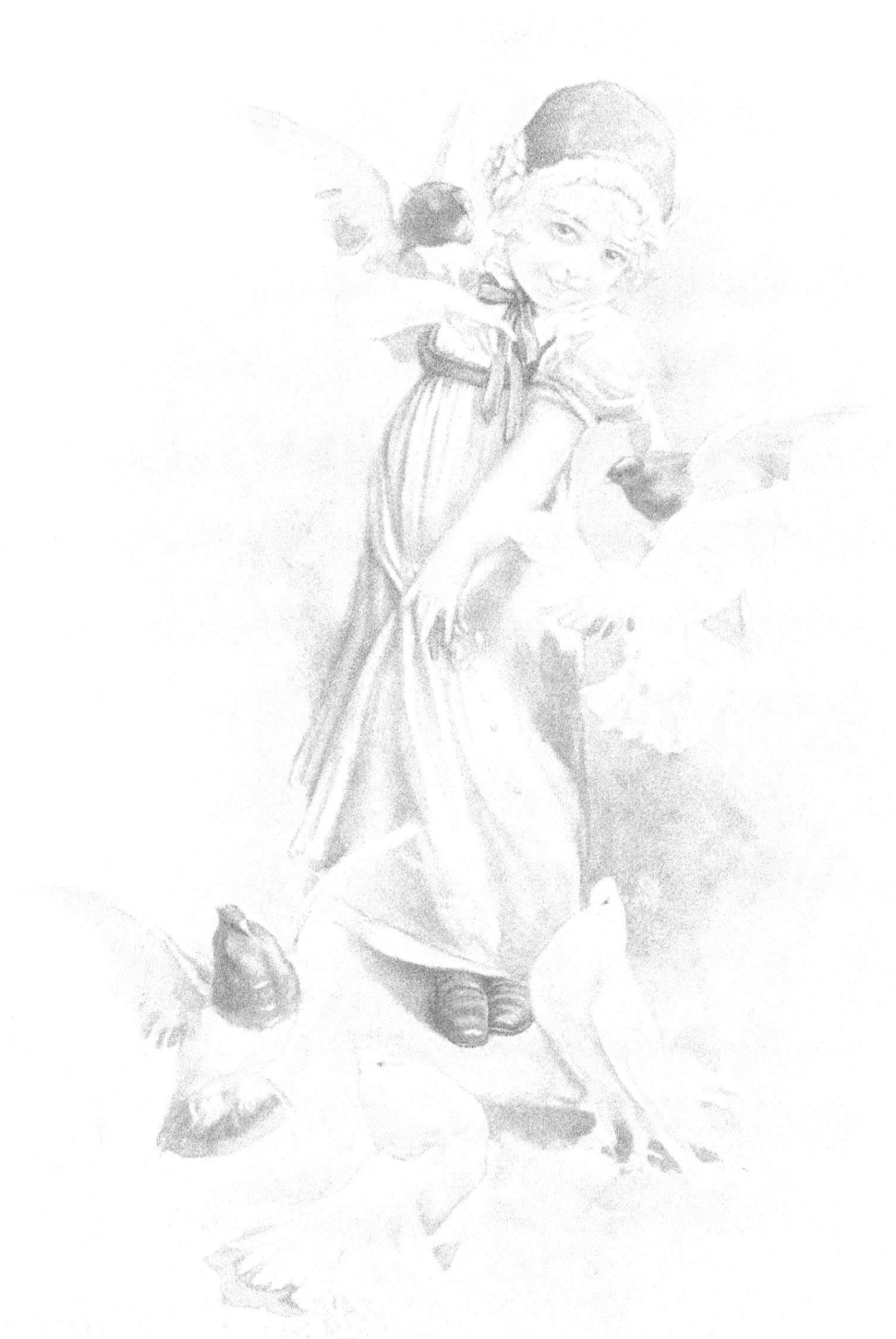

Wonderful Childhood

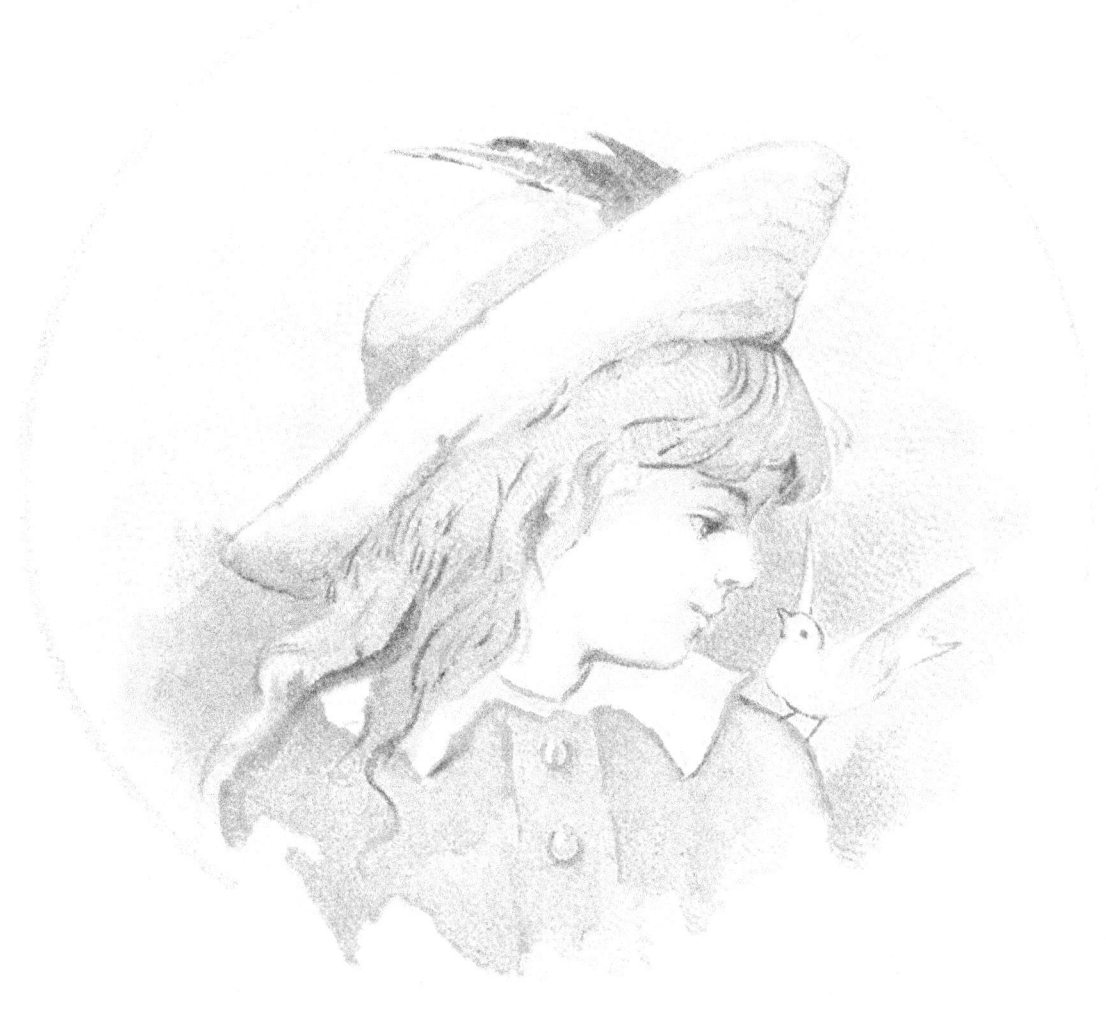

Wonderful Childhood

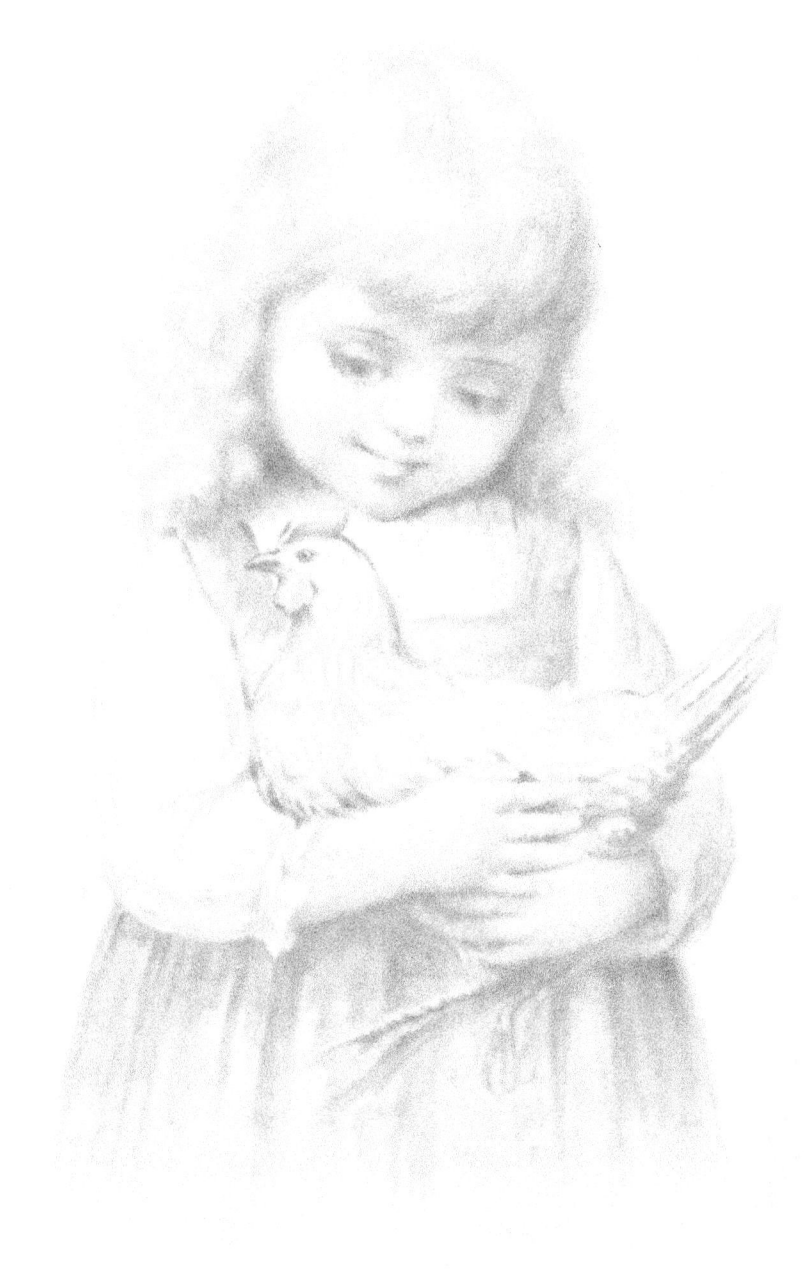

Wonderful Childhood

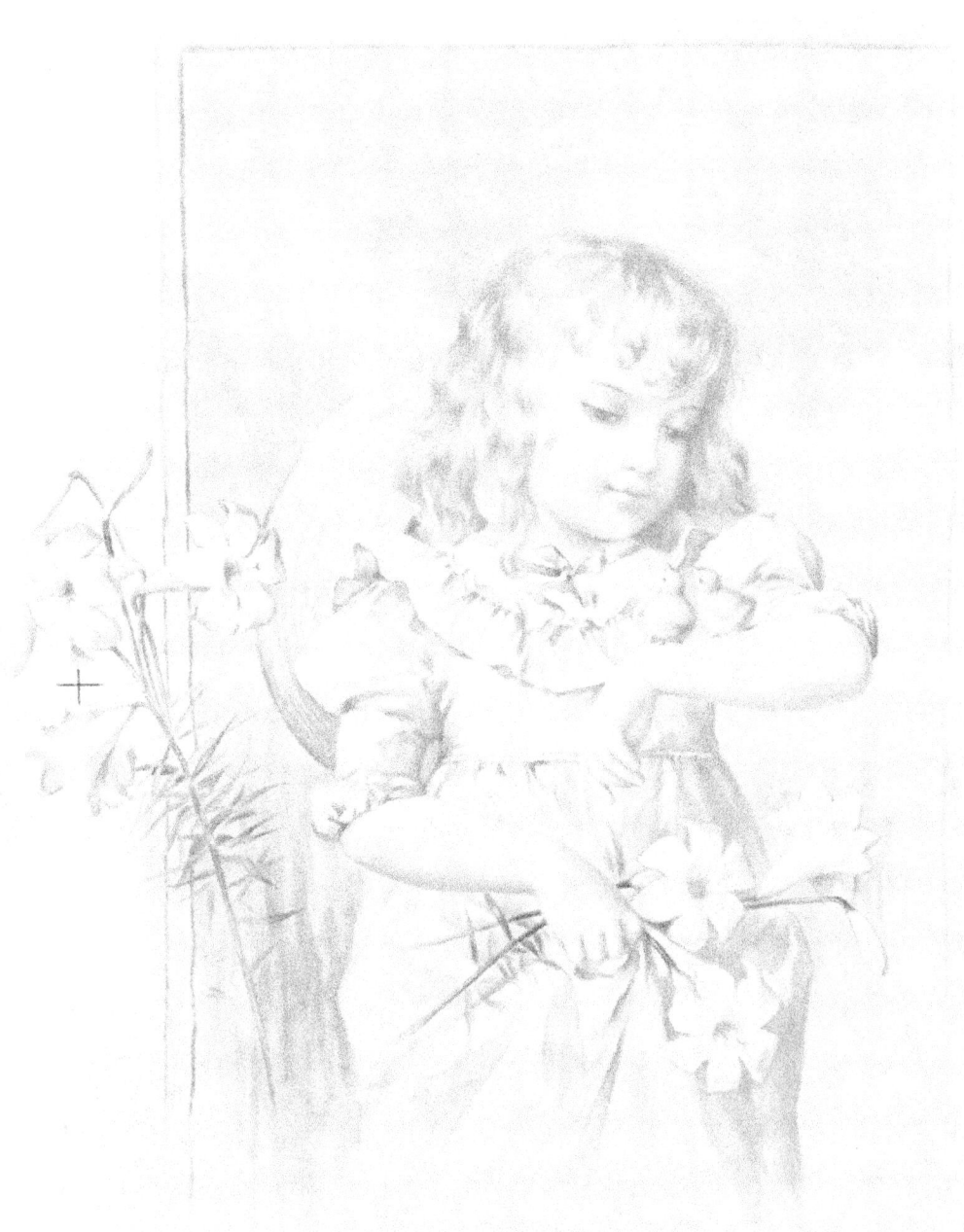

Wonderful Childhood

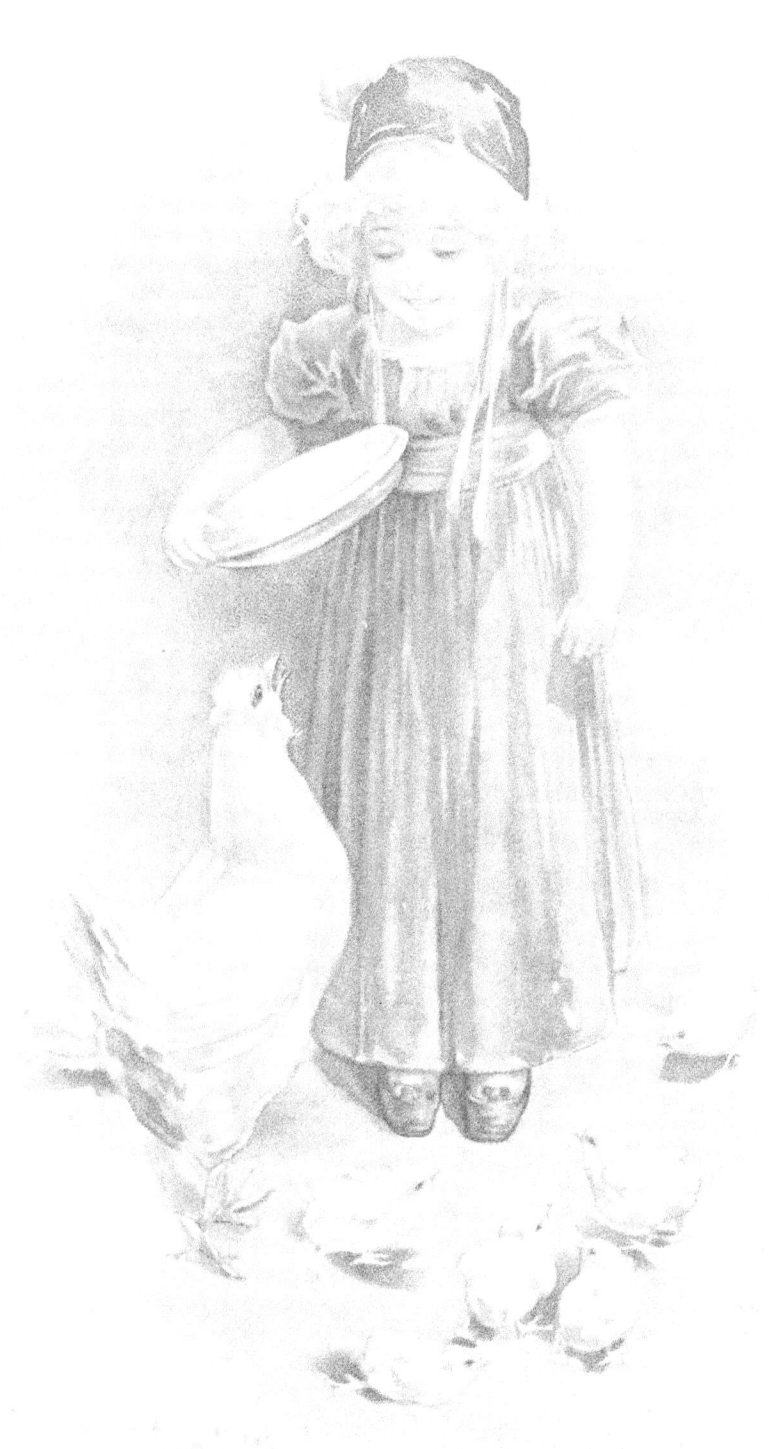

Wonderful Childhood

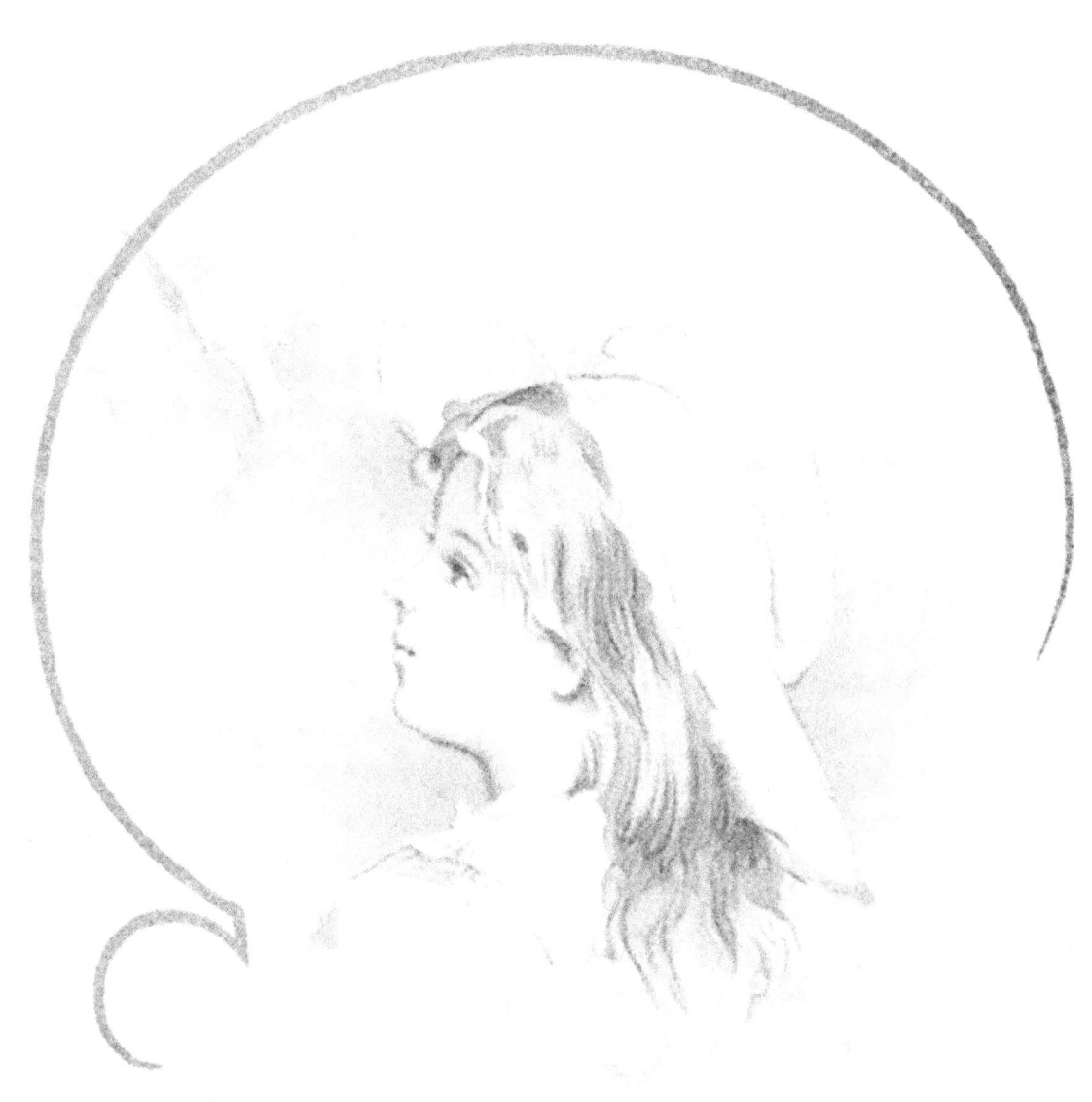

Wonderful Childhood

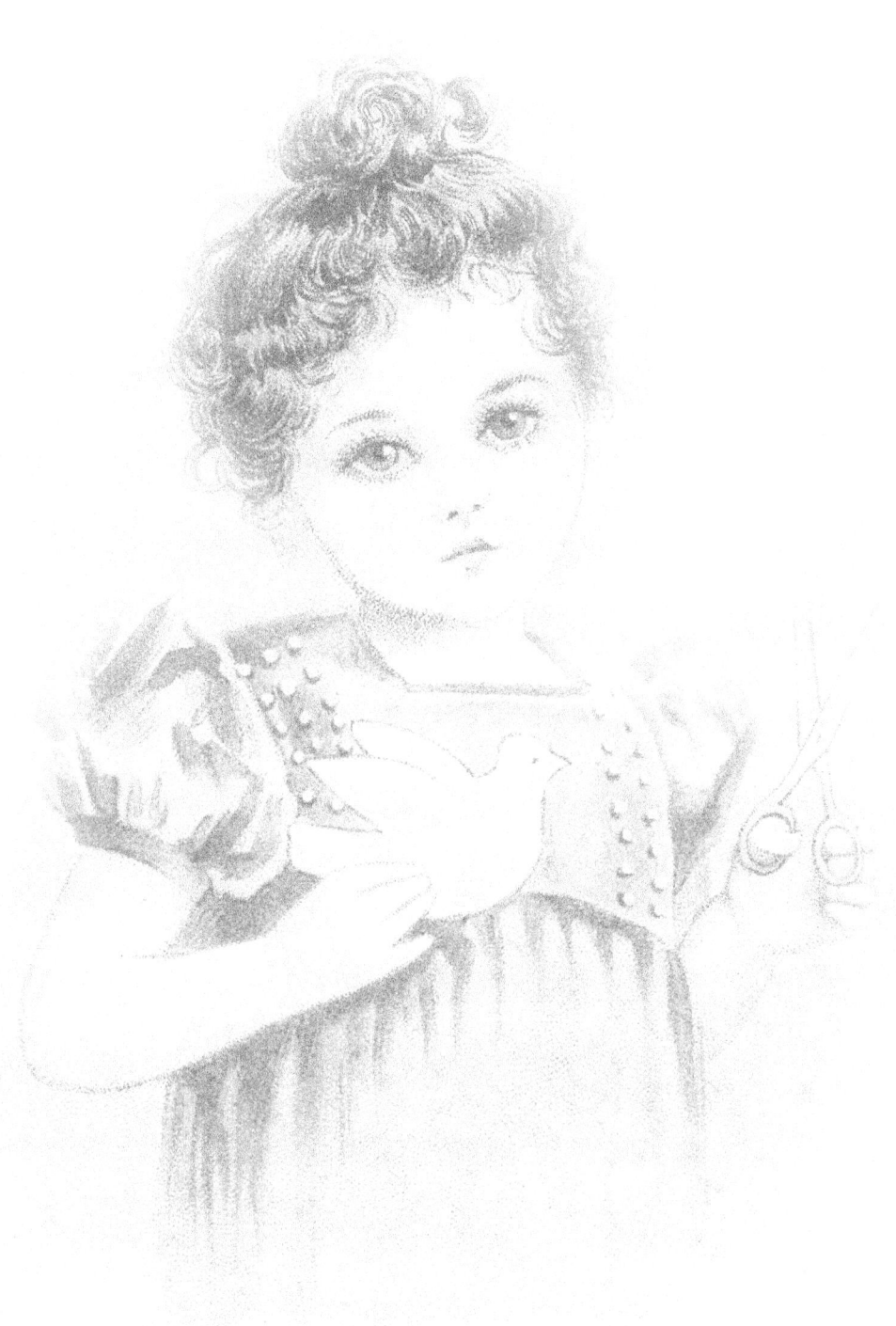

Wonderful Childhood

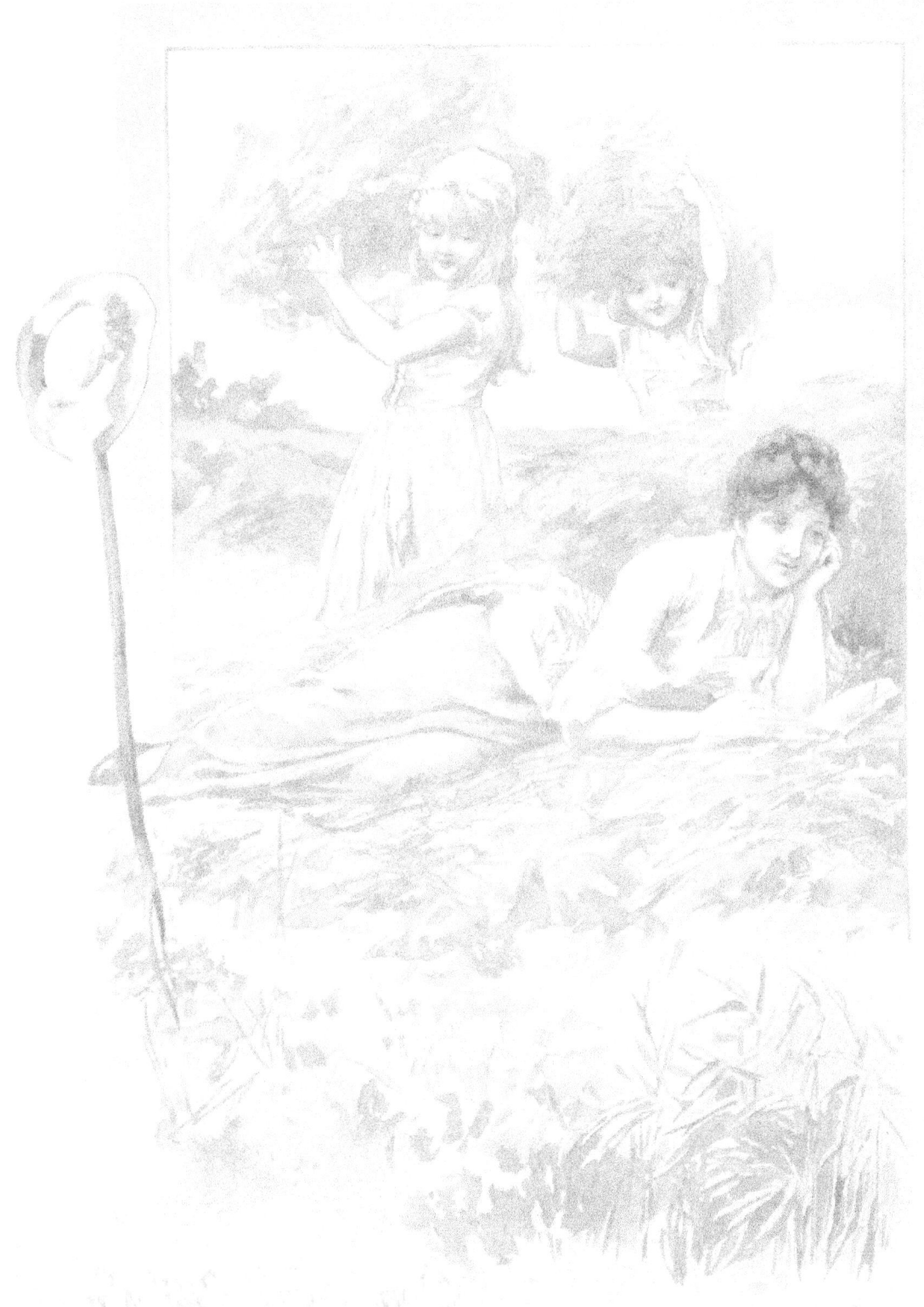

Wonderful Childhood

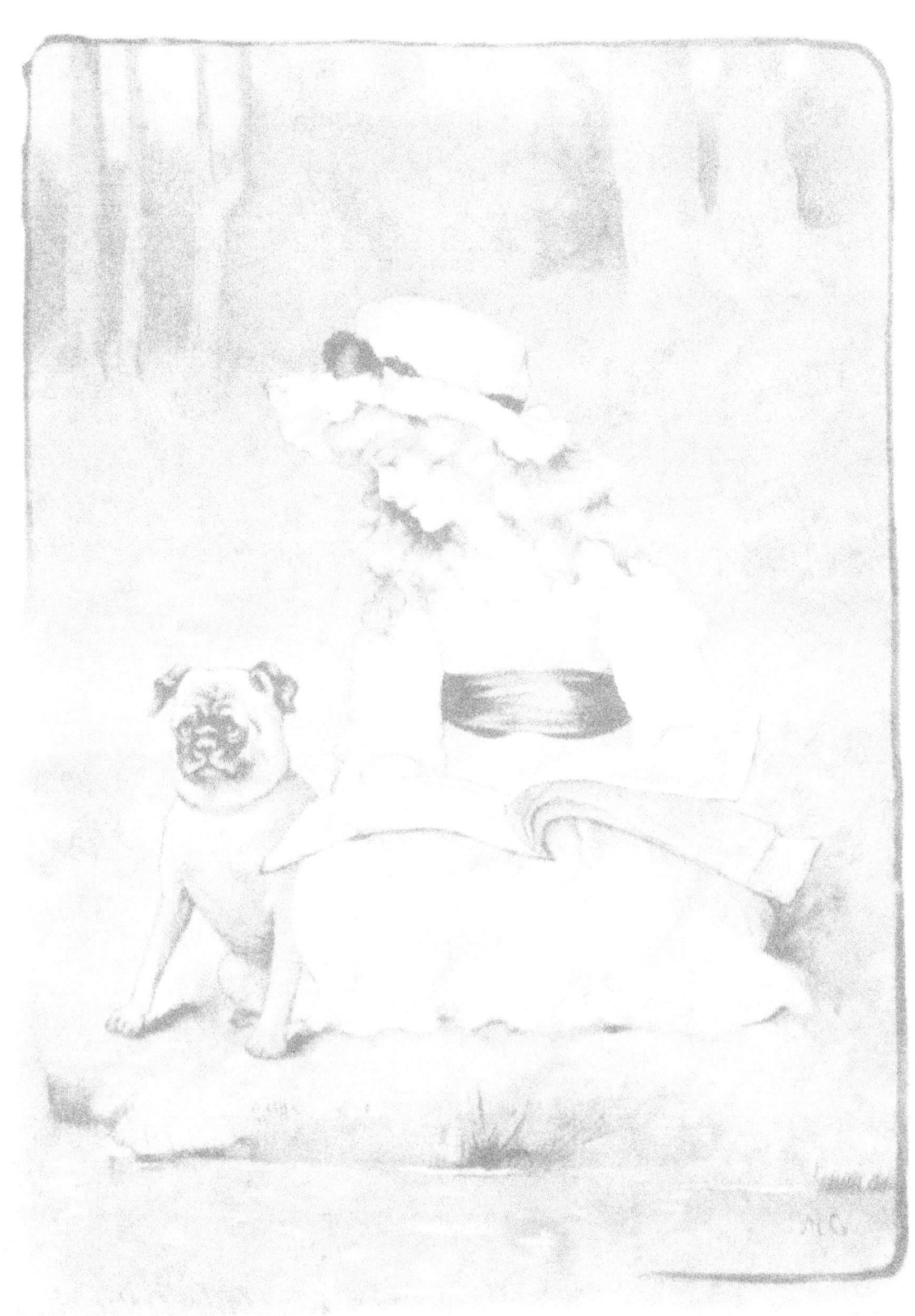

Wonderful Childhood

Wonderful Childhood

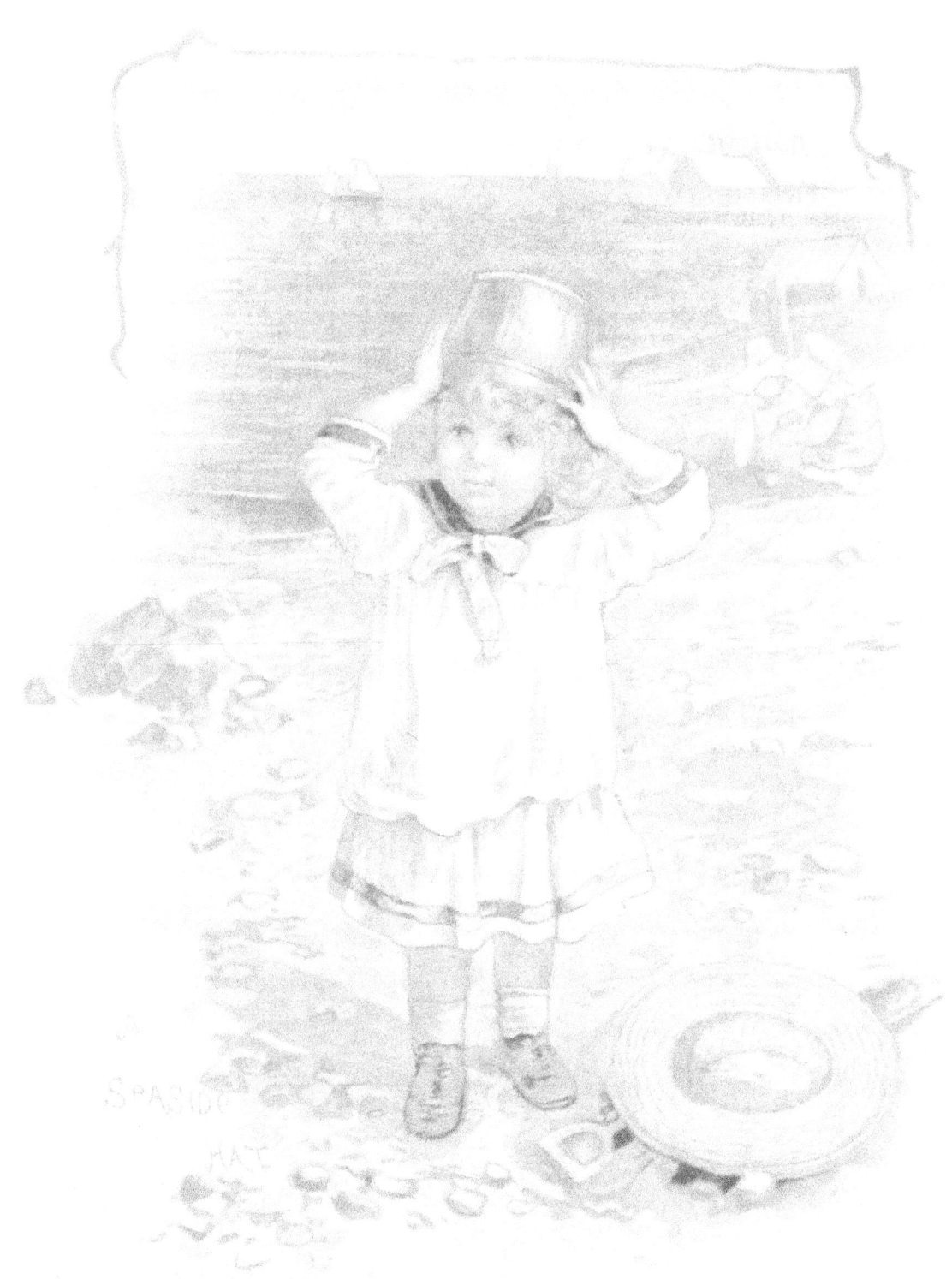

Wonderful Childhood

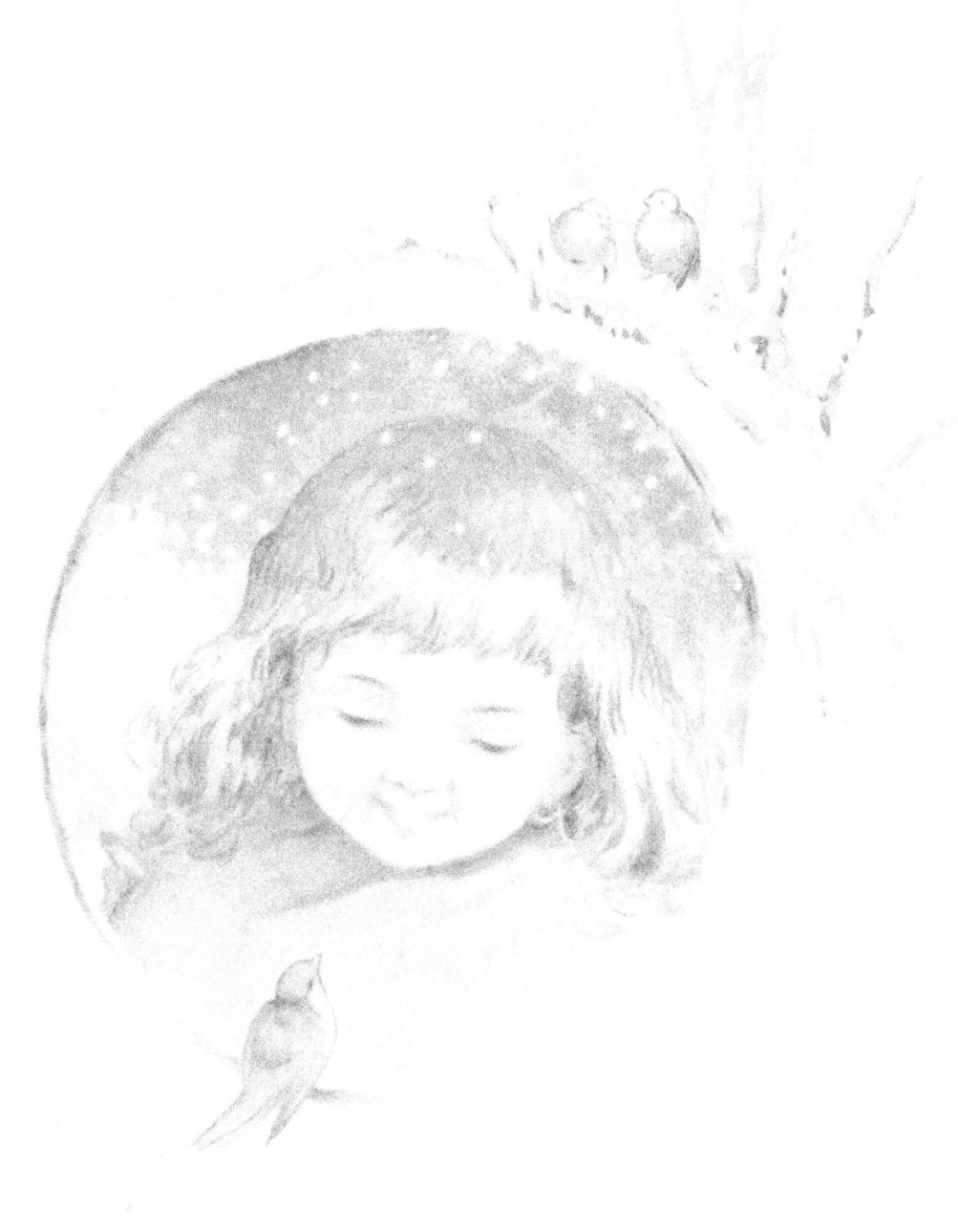